DARE TO BE DIFFERENT

ATHLETES WHO CHANGED SPORTS

BY BRAD HERZOG

A SPORTS ILLUSTRATED FOR KIDS Book

Dare To Be Different: Athletes Who Changed Sports, by Brad Herzog
A SPORTS ILLUSTRATED FOR KIDS publication/April 2000

SPORTS ILLUSTRATED FOR KIDS and KiDS are registered trademarks of Time Inc.

Cover and interior design by Emily Peterson Perez
Cover photographs: Richard Mackson/Sports Illustrated (Julius Erving), V.J.
Lovero/Sports Illustrated (Jim Abbott), John W. Zimmerman (Wilma Rudolph)

Dare To Be Different: Athletes Who Changed Sports is published by SPORTS
ILLUSTRATED FOR KIDS, a division of Time Inc. Its trademark is registered in the
U.S. Patent and Trademark Office and in other countries. SPORTS ILLUSTRATED
FOR KIDS, Sports Illustrated Building, 135 West 50 Street, 4th floor, New York,
N.Y. 10020-1393

For information, address: SPORTS ILLUSTRATED FOR KIDS

ISBN 1-886749-95-7

Printed in the United States of America

10 9 8 7 6 5 4 3 2 1

Dare To Be Different: Athletes Who Changed Sports is a production of SPORTS
ILLUSTRATED FOR KIDS Books: Cathrine Wolf, Assistant Managing Editor; Emily
Peterson Perez, Art Director; Amy Lennard Goehner (Project Editor) and
Margaret Sieck, Senior Editors; Sherie Holder, Associate Editor; Kathleen Fieffe,
Reporter; Robert J. Rohr, Copy Editor; Erin Tricarico, Photo Researcher; Ron
Beuzenburg, Production Manager

CONTENTS

DEDICATION

To Amy, who continues to dare

introduction

It takes a lot of talent to be a great athlete. You have to be able to do things like run or swim the fastest or jump the highest. But some athletes show us something even more impressive than superior skills. They display amazing courage or imagination. You will read about such individuals in *Dare to be Different: Athletes Who Changed Sports.*

In the first section of the book, we profile athletes who dared to be first. They are people like Jackie Robinson, the first African-American major league baseball player in the 20th century. If Jackie hadn't broken baseball's color barrier, in 1947, would Ken Griffey, Junior, be slugging away today? Where would tennis champion Martina Hingis be today if Billie Jean King hadn't proved that women deserve equal respect? Without these trailblazers, many of today's superstars might not be playing at all.

In the second section of the book, we present athletes who introduced different methods of playing the games. Many of today's accepted techniques in sports were the result of one person's imagination. You'll read about athletes such as Bobby Orr, the big scoring force who changed the way defensemen play hockey. Or Olga Korbut, the tiny gymnast who dazzled the world with moves no one had ever seen.

All of the athletes profiled in this book have left their imprint on sports. They all dared to be different!

JACKIE ROBINSON

The first African-American modern major leaguer was a model of courage, class, and character

Believe it or not, what may have been the most important moment in sports history occurred during a pre-season minor league baseball game. It happened on April 18, 1946, in Jersey City, New Jersey, during a game between the Montreal Royals and the Jersey City Giants. The moment came in the first inning — when 27-year-old Jackie Robinson stepped up to the plate for his second at-bat.

There were 50,000 fans in the stadium because this wasn't your ordinary baseball game. This was Jackie's first game for the Royals, who were the Brooklyn Dodgers' top minor league team. Because Jackie was an African American, this was a historic first for everybody.

It had been 58 years since the previous black man, catcher Moses Fleetwood Walker, had played for a big-league baseball team or one of its minor league clubs. Since 1889, an unwritten rule had created a "color barrier" that prevented black players from taking the field. Baseball called itself the national pastime, but major league baseball didn't give everyone a fair chance to play.

So why wasn't Jackie's first at-bat of the game the most important moment? Because he had grounded out to the shortstop. Jackie knew that he had to do better than that. He had to show the fans, the players, and the entire sports world that he could succeed. He needed to play the game of his life.

If anyone could do it, Jackie could. He was a tremendous all-around athlete who had starred in basketball, football, and track and field at the University of California at Los Angeles. After college, he spent three years in the U.S. Army. Then he set his sights on a professional baseball career. He competed in the Negro National League, one of the pro leagues in which blacks could play.

Grace under pressure

But someone special had his eye on Jackie. That was Branch Rickey, the president of the Brooklyn Dodgers. Mr. Rickey was searching for the right person to become the first black player in the modern major leagues. This person had to have more than outstanding baseball skills. He had to be smart, proud, and, above all, courageous. Jackie was perfect for the role.

Mr. Rickey signed Jackie to a contract after the 1945 baseball season and sent him to play for the Dodgers' minor league farm club in Montreal. Suddenly, Jackie was more than just a baseball player. He was a symbol of equality and hope for millions of black Americans.

Imagine the pressure! Many sportswriters wondered if Jackie was good enough for big-time baseball. One predicted that Jackie only had a one-in-a-thousand chance of succeeding. Jackie knew he had to excel, and he had to do it quickly. Otherwise, it might be a long time before another black player received an opportunity to break the color barrier.

So what did Jackie do in his fateful second at-bat that day? He hit a three-run home run! And he didn't stop there. Jackie collected four hits, four runs, and two stolen bases in that first game. Talk about grace under pressure!

Jackie went on to lead the league in runs, with 113, and batting average, .349. He also led the Royals to the league championship. Most impressive of all, he did it while suffering through insults and taunts, from racist fans, and beanballs and spikings, from opposing players. Branch Rickey had asked him to "turn the other cheek" and just play good baseball. Jackie gritted his teeth and did just that.

Welcome to the big leagues

When Jackie moved up to the Dodgers the following spring, there were rumors that many players didn't want him on the team. But Dodger manager Leo Durocher told them, "I don't care if a guy is yellow or black, or if he has stripes. I'm the manager, and I say he plays."

Jackie played beautifully. He batted .297, scored 125

runs, and led the National League with 25 stolen bases. The racist taunts and insults were even worse than those in the minor leagues, but they didn't stop Jackie. No one had ever played under more difficult conditions than Jackie played that season, yet Jackie earned the Rookie of the Year award.

Jackie spent 10 years with the Dodgers, playing mostly second base. He batted .311 and led the Dodgers to six National League championships and a World Series title. In 1949, he became the first African American to win the National League Most Valuable Player award. Thirteen years later, he was the first black player elected to the Baseball Hall of Fame.

By then, every major sports league in the country had opened its doors to African-American athletes. In fact, black baseball stars like Willie Mays, Hank Aaron, and Ernie Banks were dominating the National League. They knew Jackie was the one who got them there.

Jackie had dared and delivered.

SHIRLEY MULDOWNEY

This very fast lady gave the boys a run for their money in the high-speed world of drag racing

D rag racing is not for wimps. In drag racing, you strap yourself into a 25-foot-long car that looks like a rocket ship on wheels. Then you try to zoom over one fourth of a mile at a speed of more than 320 miles per hour! It's the fastest five seconds in sports.

For Shirley Muldowney, those are also the most exciting seconds in sports. That's why she ignored barriers and overcame obstacles to become the fastest woman on wheels! Shirley is no wimp.

"I love drag racing," she once said. "And I love beating the boys at a game they think is their own!"

Shirley faced a lot of discrimination as a woman. When she first tried to compete as a drag racer, the governing organization stalled in giving her a license. But Shirley persisted and eventually she got her license.

Soon, Shirley wasn't just competing in races, she was winning them! And she wasn't racing just any dragsters. She was racing the fastest dragsters. In 1967, Shirley became the first woman licensed by the National Hot Rod Association (NHRA) to drive Top Fuel dragsters.

(Top Fuel cars are the fastest accelerating wheel-driven vehicles in the world.) In 1976, she became the first woman to win a national event.

Clearly, Shirley had the skills. One of her great strengths was that she seemed to react quicker than her opponents to the flash of the green GO light. In a race measured in seconds, that head start is everything.

Shirley quickly became one of the most popular and famous drivers in drag-racing history, not only because she was a woman, but also because she was a champion. In 1977, she became the first woman to win an NHRA Winston championship. The Winston is a national championship in which points are awarded for finishes throughout a season. It is considered the most important title because the NHRA is the largest sanctioning drag-racing association in the world.

Winning the title again in 1980 and 1982 made Shirley the first three-time winner in drag-racing history. She also won the 1981 American Hot Rod Association (AHRA) world championship.

The one and only

Through 1999, Shirley was the only woman to have won a professional drag-racing world championship. She was also the first to win the premier event in drag racing, the NHRA U.S. Nationals. Through 1999, no other woman had won that, either.

In all, Shirley was named to the Auto Racing All-America Team seven times.

In 1983, a movie called *"Heart Like a Wheel"* was made about Shirley. Her career almost ended with a heart-stopping crash the next year. On June 29, 1984, Shirley was competing in a qualifying race when the inner tube in her left front tire popped out. Her car went off the road into a ditch at nearly 250 miles per hour. The car broke into pieces. Shirley bounced and flew about 600 feet while strapped into the driver's seat!

JANET GUTHRIE AND LYN ST. JAMES
They blazed a trail for fast women

For decades, the race starter had begun the famous Indianapolis 500-mile race by saying, "Gentlemen, start your engines." But in 1977, he said, "In company with the first lady ever to qualify, gentlemen, start your engines."

That lady was Janet Guthrie. She began her racing career in 1961, but when she qualified for the 1977 Indy 500, she became world famous. Engine trouble forced Janet out of the race early, but the next year, she completed all 500 miles and finished ninth out of 33 drivers.

A decade later, in 1987, another female driver, Lyn St. James, was part of the winning team at the famous 24 Hours of Daytona. She won the race again in 1990. Lyn finished eleventh in the 1992 Indy 500 and was the race's Rookie of the Year. In 1993, she started the Lyn St. James Foundation, which teaches young girls how to be race-car drivers. Lyn is helping to create more Janet Guthries and Shirley Muldowneys.

Shirley was severely injured. She broke bones in five of her fingers. She suffered a broken pelvis. Her legs were shattered, too. It was 15 months before Shirley could even walk again, but she had one goal in mind: She wanted to race again. Eighteen months after the accident, Shirley was back in the driver's seat. She was named the 1987 Comeback Driver of the Year.

The four-second club

In 1989, Shirley broke the five-second barrier and became one of only 16 drivers in the four-second club. Shirley went on to become the first driver ever to break five seconds in three straight national events. The next year, she became the first woman, and only the second drag racer, ever inducted into the Motorsports Hall of Fame.

As Shirley got older, she reduced the number of events in which she competed. But slowing her schedule didn't slow her driving down at all. In 1998, at the age of 58, she set an International Hot Rod Association record by covering a quarter of a mile in 4.696 seconds at 312.5 miles per hour!

Even as she approached 60 years of age, the fastest woman on wheels showed no signs of wanting to slow down.

"I still have the same 'Let's go out and beat on 'em!' attitude," said Shirley, "and as long as I have that, I want to race."

BO JACKSON

Bo knew greatness in two pro sports at the same time

The New York Yankee pitcher, Neal Heaton, peered toward home plate. There stood big Bo Jackson. Bo had once been called the greatest athlete in the world. He had been a star in the major leagues and in the NFL. But that was before he severely injured his left hip while playing football. Now doctors said he might not be able to play at all.

So what was Bo doing standing at the plate, staring down the pitcher on this day, April 9, 1993? It was 18 months since the injury. He hadn't swung a bat in a major league game in a year. Could he possibly come back and shine like the Bo of old?

Neal Heaton delivered the pitch, and the ball streaked toward Bo . . .

Mr. Everything

In the late 1980's and early 1990's, it seemed as if Bo Jackson could do everything. At his high school, in McCalla, Alabama, he was a fantastic all-around athlete. He set state track-and-field records in the high jump, long jump, hurdles, and sprints. In football, he gained 1,173 yards on 108 carries and scored 17 touchdowns as a senior. On the baseball diamond, he smashed a national-record 20 home runs and batted .447 as a senior. He even pitched two no-hitters!

The New York Yankees drafted Bo in 1982, but he decided to accept an athletic scholarship to Auburn University. He played baseball there, but he gained national attention as an unstoppable running back for Auburn's football team. After rushing for 1,786 yards in 1985, Bo won the Heisman Trophy as the best college football player in the country.

Between 1985 and 1987, Bo was drafted by two more major league baseball teams and two pro football teams. He was also drafted by a team in the International Basketball Association, even though he had never played organized basketball! Bo was such an outstanding athlete that people thought he could do anything.

Making the grade: an All-Star and Pro-Bowler

That's when Bo made a daring decision. He decided to play two professional sports at the same time. Between 1987 and 1990, he played baseball for the Kansas City Royals, from April through October, then played football for the Los Angeles Raiders, from October through January.

Bo wasn't the first two-sport athlete in history, but he surely was one of the best. In 1989, Bo hit 32 homers and knocked in 105 runs for the Royals. He was named Most Valuable Player of the All-Star Game.

Then Bo switched uniforms and gained 950 yards in only 11 games with the Raiders. He was named to the Pro Bowl the following year.

A devastating injury

In a January 1991 NFL playoff game, Bo injured his hip when he was tackled by an opposing linebacker. It was a terrible injury. Bo needed hip replacement surgery, and doctors feared he might never be able to play football or baseball again. Bo retired from football, but he still wanted to play baseball. He had promised his mother before she died that he would return to baseball. The Royals, however, released Bo from the team.

But the Chicago White Sox believed in Bo. Even though he was still on crutches, they signed him to a three-year contract in April 1991. Bo spent as many as 13 hours a day working out and rebuilding his leg strength. It took two years of rehab for his hip, but finally, in April 1993, Bo made his dramatic return.

So there stood Bo, waiting for the pitch in his very first at-bat after his surgery. And what did he do? *Smack!* He hit a homer into the rightfield bleachers! Bo was the first athlete in history to play a major pro sport with an artificial hip, and he did it with style.

Bo hit 16 homers for the White Sox that season and was

named American League Comeback Player of the Year. He retired from baseball two years later, but the memory of Bo's feats on the field and his courageous comeback will live on in the hearts and minds of sports fans forever.

DOUBLE DARES
Athletes who played two pro sports are rare

It's not easy to rank among the top professional athletes in one sport. But in two sports? That takes super all-around talent. Three athletes performed this feat in football and baseball. Bo Jackson did it from 1987 to 1990. In the 1990's, speedy Deion Sanders became one of the top cornerbacks in NFL history and also spent several seasons playing major league baseball. And Jim Thorpe (see page 33) was a football star, a major leaguer, and an Olympic track-and-field champion.

Several men played both major league baseball and NBA basketball. Ron Reed, Gene Conley, and Dave DeBusschere did it in the 1960's. Danny Ainge did it in the 1980's, but he quit baseball before trying pro basketball.

Other athletes started second careers in different sports after completing amazing careers in their first sport. Track legend Babe Didrikson Zaharias and tennis champion Althea Gibson took up golf. Babe even won three U.S. Open championships during her second career. Olympic speed-skaters Eric Heiden and Connie Paraskevin-Young were also world-class bicycle racers. Chris Witty recently made the transition from speed-skating to cycling, and Bonnie Blair tried it (although not as successfully as Eric and Connie) in 1989. Football star Herschel Walker became a member of the U.S. bobsled team.

Not every great athlete can be a two-sport star. Michael Jordan tried playing pro baseball in the mid-1990's, but he never made the grade. He couldn't hit a curveball!

ANN MEYERS

This basketball standout bounced by barrier after barrier

When Ann Meyers was growing up in La Habra, California, track and field was her favorite sport. She dreamed of someday becoming an Olympic high jumper. She wanted to jump high and finish first. Years later Ann did reach great heights, and she scored a lot of firsts — but she did it on the basketball court!

As a kid, Ann played many sports besides track and field: volleyball, softball, field hockey, badminton, tennis, and lots of basketball. She grew up in a hoops-happy family, and she often shot baskets with her brothers and sisters. Ann's dad and her four brothers and sisters all played. Her older brother, Dave, became a college star and led the University of California at Los Angeles (UCLA) to the 1975 NCAA tournament championship.

A first for the national team

In high school, Ann was a 5' 9" guard and a terrific all-around player. How good was she? She was good enough to become the first high school player ever to be named to the United States women's national basketball team! In

1975, after her freshman year at UCLA, that team won a gold medal at the Pan American Games and at the world championships.

The following year, the Summer Olympic Games were held at Montreal, in Quebec, Canada. For the first time, women's basketball was included as an Olympic sport. Ann was a member of the first U.S. women's basketball team to compete in the Olympics. Ann and her teammates won the silver medal.

Ann continued to rack up firsts. She was the first woman to receive a full athletic scholarship to UCLA, and the first basketball player, male or female, to be named to four Kodak All-America teams. During her four seasons at UCLA, Ann averaged 17.4 points and 8.4 rebounds per game.

Halls and headlines

In 1978, Ann led UCLA to the women's national college basketball championship by helping the team win the tournament that later became the NCAA women's basketball championship. Because of her stardom at UCLA, Ann later became — you guessed it! — the first woman elected to the UCLA Athletic Hall of Fame.

A year after graduating from UCLA, Ann achieved another first, and this one made headlines: She was asked to try out for the NBA's Indiana Pacers. She became the first woman to sign an NBA contract. Ann tried out, but she didn't make the team. The male college stars she was up against were bigger, stronger, and quicker. Still, the fact that she dared to even try inspired women athletes around the country and gave her a special place in women's sports history.

After she was cut from the team, Ann was given a job as one of the broadcasters for Pacer games. That was a first too! Before Ann, no woman had ever announced an NBA game.

Hall-of-Fame couple

Ann broadcast a dozen Pacer games. Then she got another opportunity to play professionally in the new Women's Basketball League (WBL). The WBL was a women's pro league, similar to today's Women's National Basketball Association (WNBA). But the WBL only lasted a few seasons. Ann herself lasted just one season, but it was a great one! She signed with the New Jersey Gems in 1979 and promptly won league MVP honors for the season.

After one year with the Gems, Ann went back to broadcasting. Over the next decade, she served as a commentator on every major network, covering events from the women's Final Four and NCAA softball to the Goodwill Games and the Summer Olympics. When the WNBA was formed, in 1997, Ann was chosen to be the league's on-air color analyst.

Along the way, Ann married Don Drysdale, a Hall of Fame pitcher for the Los Angeles Dodgers. When she was inducted into the National Basketball Hall of Fame, in 1993, Ann achieved one more first: she and Don became the first man-and-wife members of major sports Halls of Fame!

NANCY LIEBERMAN AND LYNETTE WOODARD
Two trailblazing hoopsters

When Ann Meyers was a senior at UCLA, two other women were also making headlines in college basketball. After graduating, each did something no female basketball player had ever achieved.

Nancy Lieberman, a 5-foot-10 guard with fancy passing moves, led Old Dominion University to two national championships in a row. She was a three-time All-America and a two-time college Player of the Year.

At the University of Kansas, 6-foot forward Lynette Woodard racked up 3,649 career points on her way to becoming a four-time All-America.

So what made Nancy and Lynette trailblazers? In 1985, Lynette became the first woman ever to play for the Harlem Globetrotters (a traveling basketball team known for its players' amazing ball handling and hilarious on-court antics). The very next year, Nancy played for the Springfield Fame, in the United States Basketball League, a men's minor league. So Nancy became the first woman to play men's pro basketball.

WILMA RUDOLPH

Neither poverty nor illness nor prejudice could stop her from becoming a track-and-field legend

Wilma Rudolph won Olympic gold medals as a sprinter, but you could say she was really a hurdler. During Wilma's run to stardom, life placed many obstacles, or hurdles, in her path. Wilma leaped over every one of them.

Hurdle No. 1: Wilma came from a poor family. She was the 20th of 22 children!

Hurdle No. 2: Wilma grew up in a time (the 1940's) and a place (Tennessee) in which black people were treated like second-class citizens. They were forced to eat in separate restaurants and attend separate schools from white people, and they didn't have many of the opportunities in life that white people had.

Hurdle No. 3: Wilma was a sickly child. When she was 4 years old, she contracted scarlet fever and double pneumonia [*noo-MOAN-yah*]. Even worse, soon after that she got a disease called "polio." The polio weakened her left leg so much that she could barely use it. Wilma had to wear a leg brace and a special shoe to help her walk.

"I remember the kids always saying, 'I don't want to

play with her. We don't want her on our team,' " Wilma said later. "I never forgot all those years when I was a little girl and not able to be involved."

Wilma didn't let these hurdles stop her from launching a spectacular athletic career. She used her determination and hard work to overcome anything that stood in her way! By age 12, she no longer needed the brace and special shoe. In high school, she was a four-time all-state basketball player and a track star. She won state titles in the 50-yard dash, 75-yard dash, and 100-yard dash. When she was only 16, Wilma made the 1956 U.S. Olympic Team and won a bronze medal in the 4 x 100-meter relay!

But Wilma's path wasn't clear yet.

Hurdle No. 4: Wilma was awarded a track scholarship to Tennessee State University. Then a series of hamstring injuries forced her to miss most of the 1958 and 1959 track seasons. The next year, 1960, started poorly, too, when she had to have her tonsils removed.

"How do you do, Mr. Robinson?"

But not all of the news was bad that year. Wilma got a chance to meet one of her heroes, Jackie Robinson. Jackie had told Wilma that he liked her style of running and really thought she had potential. The player who broke baseball's color barrier *(see page 6)* told Wilma: "Don't let anything or anybody keep you from running."

She didn't. At the Olympic Trials, in Seattle, Washington,

in July 1960, Wilma set the world record in the 200-meter run by reaching the finish line in 22.9 seconds. Then she headed to the 1960 Summer Olympics, in Rome, Italy.

Hurdle No. 5: At the Olympics, Wilma sprained her ankle the day before her first race. But after all she had been through, there was no way a little ankle pain was going to stop her. Wilma won the 100-meter dash by nearly three meters! Then she won the 200-meter sprint. Finally, she came from behind during the last leg of the 4 x 100-meter relay to lift the U.S. team to another gold medal.

Wilma Rudolph had overcome poverty, prejudice, illness, and injury to become the first U.S. woman to win three Olympic track-and-field gold medals!

A role model for the ages

The 1960 Olympics were the first Games to be broadcast on television around the globe. Wilma captivated viewers with her grace and character, and she became world famous and much beloved. She was named Associated Press Female Athlete of the Year in 1960 and 1961. Later, she was inducted into the National Track and Field Hall of Fame, the International Women's Sports Hall of Fame, and the U.S. Olympic Hall of Fame.

Women, especially African-American women, had not been given the opportunities and attention they deserved. Wilma's success, grace, and popularity showed the world that women could be great athletes and role models.

CHARLIE SIFFORD

As a black man in a white sport, he courageously battled racism to play golf, the sport he loved

Tiger Woods, the world's Number 1 golfer, is part Caucasian (white), part black, part American Indian, and part Asian. He calls himself "Cablinasian" to cover his racial origins. In the late 1990's, Tiger dominated the Professional Golf Association (PGA) Tour.

But if it weren't for Charlie Sifford, Tiger might have been a talent without a tour. Tiger told reporters in 1998, "Charlie, in my opinion, is one of the most courageous men ever to play this sport."

Charlie has been called the Jackie Robinson of golf. (Jackie, who is profiled on page 6, was the first black player in the modern major leagues.) Golf took even longer than baseball to open its doors to African Americans.

Throughout his career, Charlie had to endure a great deal of racism as he tried to make a living at the game he loved. He was barred from eating at the same restaurants and staying in the same hotels as white golfers. Even after the PGA Tour opened its membership to African Americans, he still was often harassed on the golf course by the crowds, course members, and other golfers.

Charlie turned professional in the 1940's, when African Americans were barred from the PGA. So Charlie played on the United Golfers' Association (UGA) Tour. The UGA was made up mostly of African-American pros. Charlie won the UGA National Championship six times, but he never earned more than $800. Occasionally, in the 1950's, he was allowed to compete in a PGA Tour event. In 1957, he won the Long Beach Open, which made him the first black man to win an event recognized by the PGA.

The end of the "whites only" rule – finally

In 1961, the PGA finally removed a rule saying members had to be Caucasian. By that time, Charlie was 38 years old, an age when most golfers begin to slow down. Charlie joined the PGA Tour anyway and finished among the Top 60 money winners every year through 1969. He also won two official tournaments.

"I really would like to know how good I could have been with a fair chance," Charlie once told reporters.

In 1975, Lee Elder became the first black man to compete in the famous Masters golf tournament. He knew how much he owed Charlie. "Without Charlie Sifford, there would have been no one to fight the system for the blacks that followed," Lee said. "It took a special person to take the things he took. . . . Charlie was tough."

WILLIE O'REE

He broke the color barrier in the NHL and still works to bring hockey to minorities

While golfer Charlie Sifford was breaking the PGA color barrier *(see page 25)* on grass, Willie O'Ree was breaking that barrier on the ice! On January 18, 1958, Willie became the first black man to play in the National Hockey League. Willie was born on October 15, 1935, in Fredericton, New Brunswick, Canada. Like most kids in Canada, Willie played hockey. Willie was a fast skater with a pretty good shot. In 1956, he was signed by the minor league Quebec Aces.

Despite Willie's love of the sport, he had to put up with racist taunts everywhere he went. He had lots of support from the people he played with, but not from the people he played *against*.

Willie faced another major obstacle. He was almost entirely blind in his right eye. He had been struck by a puck during the 1955-56 season, and the doctor told him he would never play hockey again. But Willie proved him wrong.

One day in 1957, while with the Aces, Willie got a letter from the Boston Bruins. The Bruins had several injured players and needed a healthy left winger. Willie joined the Bruins and appeared in two games before being sent back down to the minor leagues.

A big goal and a standing O

Three years after sending Willie down to the minors, the Bruins called him back up. Willie's first NHL goal was a memorable one. On New Year's Day, in 1961, he scored the game-winning goal for the Bruins against the Montreal Canadiens, the best team in the NHL. Willie received a two-minute standing ovation from the Boston crowd. Willie played half of the 1960-61 season with the team and had four goals and 10 assists.

Willie's NHL career was cut short. The Bruins had found out about his eye and an NHL rule at the time forbade players with eye impairments to play. The rule did not apply to the minor leagues, so when Willie was traded to the Canadiens, he was able to play for their farm system. Willie knew he was never going to play in the NHL again, but his career was far from over. After two seasons, Willie went on to star in the Western Hockey League (WHL). He led the WHL in goals in the 1964-65 season.

Willie retired from hockey in 1979 after a 22-year career. But he continues in the game, assisting the NHL in creating interest in hockey among minorities. He hosts the annual Willie O'Ree All-Star Game for minority players. Today, there are more than a dozen black players in the NHL.

ILA BORDERS

At age 10, she knew she wanted to someday play men's pro baseball – and that's what she did!

One home run can change everything. Just ask Ila *[EYE- la]* Borders. Ila was 10 years old when her dad took her to her first major league baseball game. When Los Angeles Dodger outfielder Dusty Baker whacked a home run out of Dodger Stadium, the crowd went wild. So did Ila. She decided right then that she wanted to be a big-league baseball pitcher.

Ila quit her softball team. She had been a third baseman and pitcher. She started practicing baseball with her dad. Mr. Borders had been a semi-pro pitcher (a semi-pro player earns some money, but the sport is not his or her profession). He taught Ila to pitch overhand. They practiced at ballparks near their home in California.

When Ila was 10, she joined a Little League team as a pitcher. She was the only girl on the team. Her coaches weren't sure how she would do, but Ila quickly mastered the mound. The following year she became a Little League All-Star. Her best game came a season later when she was 12. In one game, she faced 18 batters and struck out every one of them.

Ila played Little League throughout elementary and junior high schools. She made the boys' freshmen team at Whittier Christian High School. By the end of the season, she had moved up to the boys' varsity team, where she stayed for four years.

Ila got a big break when she received a baseball scholarship from Southern California College. While she was not the first woman to play on a men's college baseball team (*see box, left*), she was the first woman to *pitch* on a men's college team. She learned how difficult it can be for a woman to play on a men's team! Fans and opposing players booed her just because she was a woman.

Ila pitched well as a college freshman. But as a sophomore, she struggled because she

JULIE CROTEAU

She played first base in college and as a pro

There is another female baseball player who is part of the Baseball Hall of Fame. Her name is Julie Croteau, and her glove is on display in Cooperstown, New York.

In 1989, Julie became the first woman to play on a men's college baseball team. She played first base for St. Mary's College, in Maryland. "If a girl is as good as Julie, she deserves to be on the team," said one of her male teammates at the time.

In 1994, Julie joined the Colorado Silver Bullets, the first women's pro baseball squad to compete against men. She made only two errors in 29 games at first base, but had a puny .078 batting avergage.

When an injury ended Julie's baseball playing days, in 1995, it didn't end her baseball career. She landed a job as an assistant coach at the University of Massachusetts. That made her the first known female coach of a men's college baseball team.

had trouble pitching inside to batters. She finished the season 1–7 with a 7.20 ERA. People began to whisper that she didn't have the talent to play at the college level.

"I like people telling me I can't do something and then proving them wrong," Ila told a reporter from the *Christian Science Monitor*.

The next season, the school had a new coach who rarely let Ila pitch, so she transferred to Whittier College, in Whittier, California. In her senior year, a pitching coach for the St. Paul (Minnesota) Saints, a minor league team, saw her pitch in a game and liked what he saw. Ila mainly throws breaking balls, curveballs, and a change-up. The scout invited Ila to a tryout. Ila signed a contract with the Saints before the first game of the 1997 season. The dream she had first had at age 10 to play pro baseball had finally come true!

Stepping onto the mound and into the Hall of Fame

Ila made her minor league debut as a reliever in the third game of the season against the Sioux Falls (South Dakota) Canaries at Sioux Falls Stadium. When she stepped onto the mound, she made history. She became the first woman to play pro baseball on a men's team. The crowd gave her a standing ovation.

She was terribly nervous and plunked the first batter on the shoulder! After that batter walked to first, Ila gave up two hits. It was not a great night for Ila. She faced just those three hitters without getting one out. The next night, Ila pitched much better.

Still, Ila didn't have much of a fastball. She was never able to throw it faster than 76 miles per hour. That didn't please the Saints. After just a few weeks, they traded her to the Duluth-Superior (Minnesota) Dukes, another minor league team in Minnesota. The Dukes won the 1997 Northern League Championship.

Ila made history again a year later, on July 24, 1998. That day, she pitched six shutout innings for the Dukes in a 3–1 victory to become the first woman ever to win a men's pro baseball game. Despite that accomplishment, Ila finished the 1998 season 1-4 with a 8.38 ERA in 29 games.

The Dukes traded Ila to the Madison (Wisconsin) Black Wolf in 1999. In 15 appearances for Madison, she went 1–0, with an excellent 1.67 earned run average. She started in 12 of those 15 games.

Although Ila had shown that women can compete with men in pro baseball, she still dreamt of more. "I want to be a major league pitcher," she said.

Even if she never makes it to the major leagues, Ila has already received an honor given to few major leaguers. Her uniform hangs in the Baseball Hall of Fame. It is the uniform of a pitching pioneer: the first woman to play pro baseball on a men's team.

JIM THORPE

This rugged Native American beat long odds to become the world's best all-around athlete

Jim Thorpe was destined for greatness from the day he was born, on May 28, 1887. He was given the Indian name Wa-tho-huck, which means "Bright Path." Jim would go on to shine as an Olympic hero, a baseball slugger, and a football legend.

Jim was part Native American, a member of the Sac and Fox tribe. He grew up in an area that is now the state of Oklahoma, but it was then known as the Indian Territory. What made Jim's accomplishments so remarkable was that at the time, there were not many sports stars who were members of minorites. Opportunities were extremely rare for Native Americans and African Americans in sports. Prejudice was widespread throughout the country. Often, when minority athletes did succeed, many hateful people did their best to make them fail.

A rough start

The childhood years were very difficult for Jim. He had a twin brother who died when he was only eight, and Jim lost both of his parents when he was a teenager. Jim was very shy as a teenager, but he found a way to make a very loud statement . . . as an athlete.

At age 16, Jim went to the Carlisle Indian School, in Pennsylvania. There he discovered what sports he did well in — all of them! He was excellent at all the sports he competed in: baseball, basketball, hockey, lacrosse, swimming, rowing, bowling, golf, tennis, handball, gymnastics, and even figure skating. But his two best sports were football and track and field.

As a football player, Jim was unstoppable. In one game, he ran for five touchdowns. In another game, he intercepted four passes. In yet another, he kicked four field goals. In four years, Jim led Carlisle to a 43-5-2 record against some of the top college teams in the country.

Jim was an all-around star on the track, too. In one meet, he competed in seven events and won six gold medals and a bronze. Fans around the country were beginning to see what a special athlete he was. In 1912, at the Olympic Games, in Stockholm, Sweden, Jim proved it to the whole world.

The most amazing Olympic performance ever?

At the time, there were two Olympic competitions that required amazing all-around skills: the pentathlon (made up of five different events) and the decathlon (10 events). No athlete had ever won both events before.

No athlete until Jim Thorpe! He won three out of five pentathlon events and easily won the gold medal. Then he set a world record with 8,412 points (out of a possible 10,000) in the decathlon. That was nearly 700 points more than the silver medalist. As King Gustav V of Sweden gave Jim the gold medal, he told him, "Sir, you are the greatest athlete in the world."

Jim returned to the U.S. as an American hero. There was even a ticker-tape parade in his honor. Sadly, a few months after his return, Olympic officials took Jim's gold medals away. They had learned that Jim played baseball for $15 a week in 1909 and 1910. That made him a professional, an athlete who played sports for money. At the time, pro athletes were not allowed to compete in the Olympics.

The ultimate pro athlete

The decision made Jim terribly unhappy, but he didn't become bitter. Instead, he became the ultimate pro athlete. For several years, he played pro baseball and football at the same time. He was an outfielder for the New York Giants, Cincinnati Reds, and Boston Braves. And he was a running back and offensive end for the Canton Bulldogs. Jim helped make the Bulldogs the nation's best pro football team. Because of the Bulldog's popularity and success, Canton became the home of the Pro Football Hall of Fame. Jim was the first person elected to the Hall.

In 1920, a new pro football league hired Jim as its first president and biggest star. That league later became the National Football League (NFL). Jim played for several different teams until he was 40 years old. He organized one of those teams himself, the Oorang Indians. It was made up mostly of graduates of the Carlisle Indian School.

Jim was elected to the Pro Football, College Football, Track and Field, and National Indian Hall of Fames. But he never lived to see a wrong that was finally set right. In 1983, 30 years after Jim's death, the International Olympic Committee gave duplicates of Jim's Olympic gold medals to his family and restored Jim's name to the record books.

It was a fitting honor for Jim, whose bright path may have shone more brightly than any athlete in the history of sports.

GERTRUDE EDERLE

The first woman to swim the English Channel (in record time, too!) became a national hero overnight

Fifty years ago, many people believed that women weren't tough enough to compete in endurance sports. But with one remarkable journey, swimmer Gertrude Ederle showed the world just how tough women could be!

Gertrude was born in 1906 in New York City. She learned to swim when she was very young. At the family's summer cottage, in New Jersey, Gertrude's mother tied a rope around her waist and lowered her down into the water. At first, Gertrude dog-paddled, but within three days she was swimming. Gertrude started competing in races. By the time she was 12, she was swimming faster that any other woman. In fact, she became the youngest person ever to break a women's world record when she swam the 800-yard freestyle in 13 minutes 19 seconds.

At age 14, Gertrude showed she could swim far as well as fast. She beat 51 other competitors in a three-and-a-half-mile race. By the time she was 17, she had recorded more world records than birthdays!

She also earned a spot on the U.S. Olympic swim team and competed at the Olympic Games in Paris, France.

She won a gold and two bronze medals in relay events.

Gertrude returned to France in 1925. By then, she held 29 national and world records for distances ranging from 50 yards to half a mile. But Gertrude wanted to do something no woman had done before. She wanted to swim across the English Channel, the body of water that separates France and England. That's a distance of 21 miles!

Many men and women had tried to swim the channel, but heavy tides and choppy waves made it very difficult.

WOMEN'S MARATHON
The event made its Olympic debut in 1984 – finally!

In 1926, the same year Gertrude Ederle swam across the English Channel, Violet Percy of Great Britain also showed that women could cover long distances. Violet was the first woman to be officially timed in a marathon run. She ran it in 3 hours 40 minutes 22 seconds.

However, it wasn't until the 1984 Los Angeles Olympics that the women's marathon finally debuted. Men had been running marathons since the very first modern Olympic Games, in 1896. In 1984, American runner Joan Benoit and Norwegian runner Grete Waitz were the two favorites at the Los Angeles Olympics. They had raced against each other 11 times, and Grete had won 10 of them. But in the Olympic marathon, Joan pulled away from Grete after only 14 minutes and never looked back. Thousands of spectators cheered Joan as she raced. It had been a struggle to gain recognition for women's long-distance running. When Joan crossed the finish line, the struggle was over.

Only five men had been able to cross it. The fastest had finished in 16 hours 33 minutes.

During her first attempt, Gertrude had only six miles to go when a wave rolled over her. She stopped to spit out saltwater, but her trainer mistakenly thought she was collapsing. He told a spotter swimming alongside her to grab her, which disqualified Gertrude. She was disappointed, but she vowed to try again.

Success the second time around

The next year, on August 6, 1926, she made her second try. At 7:09 A.M., she rubbed lard and petroleum jelly all over her body, for warmth in the icy waters, and jumped in. After a short time, the winds picked up and the currents became extremely strong. The sea became so choppy that even steamship crossings were canceled!

Gertrude's trainer was worried. He told her she had to come out of the water. Gertrude's reply was quoted in newspapers everywhere. "What for?" she asked.

The heavy seas forced Gertrude to swim 35 miles just to cover the 21-mile distance. Finally, at 9:40 P.M., she walked ashore in Dover, England. She had crossed the channel from France, and she had done it in only 14 hours 31 minutes. She broke the men's record by more than two hours! Her women's record would last 35 years.

Gertrude became a hero. When she returned home to New York City, she was given a ticker-tape parade. Two million people crowded the streets to cheer her as she drove by. Unfortunately, Gertrude's swim had damaged her hearing. By 1928, she was partially deaf. But Gertrude simply turned her bad luck into good works. She spent many years teaching hearing-impaired children how to swim.

Gertrude always taught the children to have confidence in themselves. She knew firsthand the importance of believing in oneself. As she told reporters after crossing the English Channel: "I *knew* I could do it. I *knew* I would, and I *did.*"

CURT FLOOD

He challenged baseball owners to treat players fairly, and he helped make those players rich

Star baseball players in the 21st century make millions of dollars, and for that they should be very grateful. But whom should they thank?

They could thank the coaches who helped them develop their skills. They could thank the fans who pay to watch their games. They could thank the reporters and the broadcasters whose words and pictures turn them into superstars. They probably should thank all those people.

But there is one more person they should really thank. His name is Curt Flood. Curt stands tall in sports history because he stood up for what he believed. His stand started a revolution in the way baseball teams treat and pay players.

The Cardinals' sin

Curt was a baseball star himself. From 1958 to 1969, he played for the St. Louis Cardinals and was one of the top players in the National League. Curt batted over .300 five times. He scored 112 runs in 1963 and led the league with 211 hits in 1964. He also won seven Gold Glove Awards as a slick-fielding centerfielder.

But Curt is best known for what he did *off* the field. After 12 seasons with the Cardinals, Curt was traded to the Philadelphia Phillies. He found out about the trade from a newspaper reporter. He was angry. After all his years of loyal service, Curt felt someone from the Cardinals should have told him. Also, he had friends, family, and business interests in St. Louis. He didn't want to move.

Curt thought about retiring, but he was only 31 years old. Instead, he decided to challenge baseball's "reserve clause." The reserve clause meant that unless a player was traded, sold, or released, he was bound for life to the team he currently played for. He had no control over where or for whom he could play. Curt called the clause baseball's right to treat human beings like used cars.

Merry Christmas!

On Christmas Eve 1969, Curt wrote a letter to baseball commissioner Bowie *[boo-ee]* Kuhn asking for the right to consider contract offers from other teams. Commissioner Kuhn refused Curt's request, so Curt sued Major League Baseball. He wanted to become a "free agent," which meant he would be free to accept a contract from any team.

Curt was risking his career. He was up against owners, who could punish him after the ruling came down. He got death threats, was criticized in the media, and booed by fans for being selfish. Not one of the nearly 600 big-league players testified for Curt in his court case. Marvin Miller, the leader of the Baseball Players Association, said that Curt's decision to speak out against the reserve clause took as much courage as Jackie Robinson *(see page 6)* needed in his rookie season.

Curt loses, but the players win

Curt lost the case. He appealed the decision, but the U.S. Supreme Court ruled, 5–3, to keep the reserve clause.

If Curt lost, why is he so important? Even though he lost his battle, the players won the war. Thanks to the publicity surrounding the case, players, sportswriters, and fans began to agree with Curt, and the union pressed on. In 1975, two pitchers filed a grievance to have the clause removed. A federal arbitrator struck down the clause.

As soon as top players were allowed to become free agents, teams began bidding for their services. Salaries skyrocketed and stars soon were making millions.

Curt never got to enjoy a higher salary. He sat out the 1970 season while waiting for his case to reach the Supreme Court. In 1971, the Washington Senators got his rights from the Phillies. Curt played for the Senators because he had lost more than $100,000 by not playing in 1970. Curt played only 13 games and retired in 1971.

In the long run, Curt was recognized as a brave pioneer. He had put his career on the line to stand up for what he believed.

MANON RHEAUME

**This gutsy woman stopped pucks and opened eyes
in the world of men's pro ice hockey**

In hockey, the goaltender is the last line of defense. But one goalie, named Manon Rheaume *[MAN-ohn ray-OHM]*, is known for being first. Manon was the first woman to sign a professional hockey contract. She was the first woman to play in a regular-season pro hockey game. She was the first woman to play for a National Hockey League (NHL) team.

No wonder Manon has been called the First Lady of Professional Hockey!

Playing with the big boys

Manon grew up in Lac-Beauport, Ontario, in Canada. She learned to skate at age 3, and began playing hockey two years later. Often, she ended up being the goalie while her older brothers aimed shots at the net. Playing against bigger, stronger, faster players sharpened Manon's reflexes faster than if she had just played against kids her own size. Those players were good, too: One of Manon's brothers, Pascal, was so talented that he went on to play in the NHL.

As a kid, Manon never dreamt that she might make it to the NHL, too. In fact, when Manon was 10 years old, her teacher asked each student in the class what he or she would like to be when grown up. Most of the boys said they wanted to play pro hockey. Manon said she wanted to be a schoolteacher.

"The thought of making a career out of playing hockey never even crossed my mind," she said.

Breaking down barriers

Manon loved the game, but there weren't many opportunities for girls in ice hockey. Manon sometimes had to travel as far as 150 miles to play hockey with other girls. So she began playing hockey with the boys. And she soon realized she was good! At the age of 11, Manon became the first girl to compete in the International Pee Wee Hockey Tournament. She was the goaltender.

By the time Manon was 19, she was breaking down bigger barriers. Major junior hockey in Canada is a big deal. It is the training ground for many future NHL stars. And it had always been for boys only. But on November 26, 1991, Manon took her place in the goal for the Trois-Rivieres Draveurs, in a game against the Granby Bisons. Manon stopped 14 of 17 shots and quickly earned the respect of the other players.

The next season, Manon was asked to try out for the Tampa Bay Lightning, an NHL team! She made history again by tending goal in a pre-season game against the St. Louis Blues on September 23, 1992. Manon stopped seven of nine shots in one period of play, but she gave up two goals the next period.

"I faced a lot of obstacles, not to mention a lot of pucks, to get there," said Manon. "But my determination to keep playing, even though a lot of people tried to convince me to stop, made me a much stronger person."

Manon was cut from the Lightning roster before the regular season began. But right after camp was over, she signed a three-year contract with the Atlanta Knights of the International Hockey League, a minor league.

On December 13, 1992, in a contest against the Salt Lake Golden Eagles, Manon became the first woman to play in a regular-season professional hockey game. She stopped three shots and allowed one goal in nearly six minutes of play.

All kinds of hockey

After that, Manon played on men's teams in leagues from New Jersey to Nevada. She played pro roller hockey and became the first female goalie to win a pro hockey game on wheels.

Manon didn't forget about the women, either! She played for Canada's national women's ice hockey team and won gold medals at the 1992 and 1994 world championships. When women's hockey made its debut at the 1998

Winter Olympics, in Nagano, Japan, she helped the Canadian team earn a silver medal.

Manon may not have become the schoolteacher she predicted, but her career is a lesson in determination.

"It has never been easy," said Manon. "But I've always wanted to play hockey. I'd rather play hockey than do anything else. If you have that kind of desire, I think you can achieve what you want to achieve."

CHARLINE LABONTE
Following in Manon's skatesteps

Manon Rheaume may have been the first female to play Canadian major junior hockey, but she wasn't the first female player drafted. That honor belongs to Charline Labonte, and it didn't happen until June 1999.

Charline was a 17-year-old goaltender when she was drafted by the Acadie-Bathurst Titans. The Titans play in the Quebec Major Junior Hockey League, which has sent several goaltenders to the NHL, including Patrick Roy and Martin Brodeur.

But Charline's road to the NHL looked like quite an uphill battle. The Titans were a last-place team, and she was the team's backup goalie. Still, her coach said, "She has very good technique, and she's very smart."

As a female goalie in an all-male league, Charline often received some interesting attention. Opposing players even tried to flirt with her in front of the net! But Charline kept her mind on the game. She turned back the flirts by turning back their shots!

JIM ABBOTT

This powerful pitcher didn't let a missing hand make him miss his major league dream

When Jim Abbott was growing up, in Flint, Michigan, he dreamed of being called a major leaguer. Instead, kids called him "crab."

Those kids were mean. They called Jim crab because of the way his right hand looked. Jim was born without a right hand. He wore a prosthesis, a device that performed some functions of his missing hand. Some of the kids thought the prosthesis looked strange and they called him names like crab or Captain Hook. After a while, Jim stopped wearing the prosthesis.

But he didn't stop dreaming. Jim didn't let other people's cruelty — or his handicap — keep him from working toward his goal. So what if he didn't have two hands? He would become a baseball star using just one.

"A few people told me that I wouldn't go far in sports," said Jim. "I didn't listen."

Jim pitched with his left hand. But he also had to wear his fielding glove on that hand. So he would hold the glove in the crook of his right elbow and then slip it onto his pitching hand quickly after he pitched the ball. As soon as he fielded the ball, he would cradle the ball and glove in the crook of his right arm, grab the ball with his left hand, and throw it.

These sound like complicated moves, but Jim learned to do them in the blink of an eye. In fact, he became a very good fielder. Once, eight batters in a row bunted on him during a high school game, trying to take advantage of his handicap. He threw out seven of them! Jim's blazing fastball got plenty of the other batters out.

But Jim was more than a great pitcher. Jim became an all-around star in high school. He played first base, shortstop, and leftfield, and he swung a mighty bat. In his senior year, he hit .427, with seven homers and 31 runs batted in! Oh, yeah, he was also the starting quarterback and punter on the high school football team!

The nation's best amateur athlete

In 1985, Jim was selected by the Toronto Blue Jays in the 36th round of baseball's free-agent draft. But he decided to attend the University of Michigan instead of turning pro. There, he posted a 26–8 pitching record over three seasons and earned the 1987 James E. Sullivan Memorial Award as the nation's top amateur athlete.

Jim's college success earned him a spot on the U.S. Olympic Baseball Team. At the 1988 Summer Games, in Seoul, South Korea, baseball was a demonstration sport, and Jim put on a demonstration of his own! He pitched the

U.S. to victory over Japan in the championship game, to earn a gold medal.

In 1988, Jim was selected again in the free-agent baseball draft. This time, the California Angels chose him in the *first* round. Jim leaped straight to the major leagues without playing in the minors, and he won 12 games in his rookie season!

The best season of Jim's career came in 1991, when he was 18–11, with a 2.89 earned run average for the Angels. Two years later, pitching for the New York Yankees, Jim achieved the highlight of his career. On September 4, 1993, he tossed a no-hitter against the Cleveland Indians. The feat made headlines throughout the country.

A fighting spirit

Over the next six years, Jim pitched for the Chicago White Sox, the Milwaukee Brewers, and the Angels. He lost more games (108) than he won (87) during his career, but he never lost sight of his most important job: being a role model for kids and adults with disabilities. In 1995, Jim received the Hutch Award, which is given each year to a major leaguer with character and a fighting spirit.

What satisfied Jim most, though, was that people no longer viewed him as a one-handed pitcher. They saw him as a *left-handed* pitcher. That happened because Jim dared to dream. "I believe you can do anything you want," he said, "if you put your mind to it."

THEY OVERCAME
Physical disabilities didn't stop these stars

Through the years, many major league baseball players have overcome physical disabilities to become stars.

Mordecai Brown was known as "Three Finger" because he injured his right hand when he was 7 and lost the use of two fingers. He still won 239 games as a right-handed pitcher and was elected to the Hall of Fame.

Another pitcher, Hugh Daily, was nicknamed "One Arm." He threw a right-handed no-hitter in the 1880's after losing his left hand in a gun accident.

Then there was the case of William Hoy. William played in the major leagues from 1888 to 1902. He was thoughtlessly nicknamed "Dummy" because he was deaf. He turned out to be one of the best centerfielders of his time.

William led the league with 82 stolen bases in his rookie season. The next year, he set a major league record by throwing out three base runners at home plate in one game. In his 14-year career, he batted .288 and recorded 597 stolen bases.

Perhaps most important, William developed a system of hand signals to communicate with his teammates and coaches. Many people believe that these evolved into the hand signals used by umpires today.

HASSIBA BOULMERKA

Algeria hasn't been the same since she defied Muslim tradition and raced to Olympic glory

Few Olympic athletes have shown more courage than Hassiba Boulmerka *[bull-MERK-uh]*.

Hassiba was born in Algeria, a country in northern Africa. It wasn't easy for Hassiba to grow up as a talented female runner there. Islam is the main religion in Algeria. The followers of Islam, called Muslims, have very strong beliefs concerning women and their appearance. Strict Muslims believe that when women are in public, they should be covered from head to toe. Imagine trying to run in all those clothes!

Many Muslims also believe that women should not be athletes. As recently as 1989, a large group of Algerians wanted to ban women from playing any sports at all!

Sometimes, as Hassiba jogged along the roads, men who saw her in her running shorts spat or threw stones to show how they felt about her and what she was doing! Hassiba just ignored them and kept running.

In 1988, Hassiba competed at the Seoul Olympics. She failed to advance past the first round in the 1,500 meters, so she and her coach decided to make a four-year plan.

They aimed for gold in the 1992 Barcelona Olympics. Hassiba knew it would take time and much practice to reach her goal.

"You can't be a champion in a week or a year. You must accept a time of suffering," she said.

Hassiba didn't suffer long. In 1991, she won the world championship in the 1,500-meter run. She was the first woman from an African or Arabic country to win a world track title. After she won, she was so happy that she screamed . . . and screamed . . . and screamed.

"I was screaming for joy and for shock," Hassiba told reporters when she finally calmed down enough to explain. "I was screaming for Algeria's pride and Algeria's history and still more. I screamed, finally, for every Algerian woman, every Arabic woman."

A symbol for women around the world

Hassiba became a symbol for women all over the world who wished for more freedom in their society. When Hassiba returned home, a parade was held in her honor. "You did what we haven't been able to do for years," several political leaders told Hassiba. "You brought us together." (Algeria has a long history of conflict among its people.)

But there were still some people who criticized Hassiba for going against Muslim belief. Although Hassiba's shorts were more modest than the outfits worn by other runners, several religious representatives denounced her for "running with naked legs in front of thousands of men."

Hassiba answered her critics by explaining that she was a practicing Muslim but also an athlete. Traditional Islamic clothing would slow her down too much.

In 1992, it was time for Hassiba and her coach to see if their four-year plan would lead to Olympic gold. It did! At the Barcelona Games, Hassiba won the 1,500 meters to become the first Algerian — man or woman — to win Olympic gold. When the race ended, Hassiba pointed to her green-and-red uniform. "I pointed to my chest for Algeria, courage Algeria," she said. "I expressed my wishes that my Algerian brothers understand that message."

Hassiba won the 1,500-meter world championship again in 1995. At the 1996 Summer Olympics, in Atlanta, Georgia, she finished last in the semi-final race after her feet got tangled with another runner. But Hassiba received another honor during those Games. The athletes from around the world voted her one of seven Summer Olympic athletes named to the International Olympic Committee Athletes' Commission.

Hassiba is still a controversial person in her homeland. Although she has received gold medals, she has also received death threats for doing what earned those medals: running. Even so, Hassiba remains a brave voice in the struggle for equality in athletics for women around the world.

BILLIE JEAN KING

This tennis legend has spent her entire career fighting for equality for female athletes

On September 20, 1973, all eyes were on Billie Jean King as she entered the Houston Astrodome. More than 30,000 eager spectators had come to watch her play a tennis match that would become the most-watched tennis match in history. Nearly 50 million fans at home were glued to their television sets.

Back then, Billie Jean was the queen of women's tennis. She had held the Number 1 women's ranking five times between 1966 and 1972. Over her 16-year (1968-1984) career, Billie Jean would win 695 matches, including a combined total of 39 singles, doubles, and mixed doubles Grand Slam championships.

But Billie Jean was more than a terrific athlete. She believed deeply that female athletes deserved equal opportunity, equal money, and equal respect. She fought for these things during the struggle for women's rights in the 1960's and 1970's, and continues to do so today. She helped form the Women's Sports Foundation, which promotes athletic opportunities for girls and women. She persuaded her fellow players to form a players' union, the Women's Tennis Association. Today, the world's top female players earn millions of dollars playing dozens of tournaments on the WTA Tour. But that wasn't true in 1973.

That's why so many people were watching the match in the Astrodome that day. Billie Jean was about to play a match, win or lose, that would go down in tennis history. Her opponent was Bobby Riggs.

Bobby had once been one of the best tennis players in the world. In 1939, he had been the Wimbledon and U.S. champions. But now, at age 55, he was famous for his big mouth! He was always boasting that he could do something goofy, like carry a suitcase while playing a tennis match. His latest boast was that he could beat Billie Jean in a three-set match. By defeating her, he would prove that male pros are better than female pros.

Putting a big mouth in his place

The match, which was called the "Battle of the Sexes," was a rather silly spectacle. Bobby entered the stadium by riding in a Chinese rickshaw pulled by six women. Billie Jean was brought in on a throne carried by four men.

But Billie Jean knew how important a victory could be. "It was not about tennis. It was about social change," she told the media at the time.

It was also no contest. Billie Jean ran Bobby all over the court. She won the first set, 6–4. She won the second set, 6–3. And she won the third, 6–3! When it was over, Billie Jean and Bobby shook hands.

"I said a lot of things. I was wrong. I admit it," Bobby later told reporters. "I didn't choke. She beat me."

That victory only proved what Billie Jean had spent her life fighting for: women athletes deserve the same respect as male athletes. "[That match] was about changing a way of thinking, about getting women athletes accepted," Billie Jean told reporters.

Martina Navratilova, another tennis legend, spoke for thousands of women athletes, past and future, when she told reporters, "Billie Jean was a crusader, fighting a battle for all of us."

BILL RUSSELL

This intimidating tower of power put the "D" in defense and ruled the NBA for 14 years

These days, you hear people say it all the time: Defense wins championships. The best offense is a good defense. The other team can't beat you if it can't score. True superstars shine at both ends of the basketball court.

Lots of people say it, but Bill Russell *proved* it. The 6' 10" star center for the Boston Celtics really put the *D* in Defense: He was determined, dependable, and daunting. Around the basket, he could be downright terrifying. An opponent would drive to the hoop, and — *whoosh!* — Bill would swoop in and block the shot. A ball would bounce off the rim and — *wham!* — Bill would grab the rebound with lightning-quick speed.

By *D*-nying his opponents even a sniff of the basket, Bill often sent the other team down to *D*-feat. In fact, Bill may have been the greatest champion that basketball has ever seen. Between 1955 and 1969, he played a big role on teams that won two college national titles, 11 NBA titles, and an Olympic gold medal! Whenever a championship was on the line, Bill Russell was sure to *D*-liver.

Although Bill is now considered one of the greatest

players in basketball history, he was just a third-string center on his high school junior varsity team.

Bill began concentrating on his rebounding skills, and that was what turned his game around. By the time he began playing college basketball for the University of San Francisco, he was a 6' 9" defensive dynamo! He led San Francisco to back-to-back NCAA championships and a streak of 55 straight victories in 1955 and 1956. He led the United States' men's team to an easy gold medal at the 1956 Summer Olympics, in Melbourne, Australia.

The greatest team in NBA history

Bill was drafted by the Boston Celtics, and he became the key ingredient to the greatest team in NBA history. The Celtics won the NBA championship in 1957. Then, from 1959 to 1966, they won eight NBA titles in a row. The Chicago Bulls may have had a couple of "three-peats" in the 1990's, but Bill's Celtics had an "eight-peat"!

In 1966, Celtics coach and general manager Red Auerbach decided to give up coaching. He chose Bill as his replacement. That made Bill the first African-American head coach of a major U.S. professional sports team. Bill served as Boston's player-coach for three seasons and — surprise! — the Celtics won two more championships.

Bill was a true pioneer on the court. He changed the way people played basketball by demonstrating that defensive play could control a game. Bill averaged only

15.1 points per game in his NBA career, but he was still voted the league's MVP five times! Before Bill came along, no one believed that a player could dominate without being a super scorer.

Chairman of the boards

Rebounding is an important part of defense, and in this department, Bill led the NBA four times. He pulled down an astounding 21,620 rebounds in his career, averaging 22.5 per game. Once, he grabbed 51 in one game!

The NBA didn't even record an official statistic for blocked shots until after Bill retired. If it had, he probably would have led the league every year. Elvin Hayes, an opposing center who became a Hall of Famer, called Bill "the ghost" because he would "come out of nowhere to block your shot."

Following Bill, many centers built their games on the ability to strike fear in opponents who tried to drive down the middle of the court. NBA standouts Alonzo Mourning and Dikembe Mutombo are two such players.

But it was Bill Russell who was basketball's first Sultan of Swat. As his old coach, Red Auerbach, once said: "Bill put a whole new sound in pro basketball — the sound of his footsteps."

OLGA KORBUT

This little sprite of a gymnast won the hearts of the world with moves no one had ever seen

When Olga Korbut was growing up in the Belorussian Soviet Socialist Republic (now known as Belarus), she would often get into mischief. She would climb over fences and up trees, trying to help herself to some fruit. She wasn't supposed to do it, but she couldn't help it. Olga had lots of energy and no fear . . . of climbing or getting caught!

Soon Olga began to use her athletic skills for other things besides climbing fences and trees. She began attending a school with a special program for athletes. She had been chosen to attend by the government. Olga still liked to run, jump, and climb. But now she did it as a gymnast.

When Olga was 14, her gymnastics coach gained special permission for her to compete in the 1969 Soviet National Gymnastics Championships. (Usually, only athletes age 16 and older competed in the nationals.) Young Olga placed fifth in the all-around competition!

More important, she performed two moves that nobody had ever seen. She did a backward somersault on the balance beam (later nicknamed "the Korbut salto beam") and a backflip-to-a-catch on the uneven bars (the Korbut flip). Her coach had taught her these moves.

Three years later, at the 1972 Summer Olympics, in Munich, West Germany, Olga performed the Korbut flip for the first time outside of the Soviet Union. The crowd was astonished. So were the television announcers. "Has that been done before by a girl?" asked one.

"Not by any human that I know of," said the other.

Some of Olga's moves looked scary. But Olga was fearless. "Maybe it is dangerous," she told reporters, "but when you start thinking of danger, you might as well give up."

The world's darling

It wasn't only Olga's daring moves that made her stand out in Munich. At 17, she was the youngest member of the Soviet team. And, at 4' 11" and 84 pounds, she was one of the smallest athletes at the Olympics.

Fans loved Olga's beaming smile. She wasn't afraid to show her emotions when she was pleased or disappointed. During the competition for the all-around title, she was in the lead after the floor exercise and the vault.

But during her routine on the uneven bars, she stubbed her toe, lost her concentration, and slipped off the bar twice. Olga's score of only 7.5 out of 10 meant she couldn't win the all-around title. She returned to her seat and broke down in tears. Seeing Olga cry only made the millions of television spectators love her more.

The next day, Olga made a thrilling comeback in the individual competition. She won two gold medals (balance beam and floor exercise) and a silver medal (uneven bars). She added those medals to the team gold she and her Soviet teammates had won.

Too much of a good thing?

After the Olympics, Olga became a worldwide celebrity. People all over the world would ask her for her autograph. She became so well-known that crowds surrounded her wherever she went. She sometimes had to wear disguises to escape the crowds!

When Olga toured the United States in 1973, record crowds watched her perform at meets throughout the country. She was the first gymnast ever named Associated Press Female Athlete of the Year.

By 1976, at age 21, Olga was one of the older gymnasts at the Olympic Games, in Montreal, Canada. But she added to her medal haul with another team gold medal and a silver medal on the balance beam.

By then, it was already clear that her fame had created a new generation of gymnasts throughout the world. They were younger and smaller and more acrobatic. They did difficult flips and acrobatic moves introduced by the person they all wanted to be: Olga Korbut.

JAN BOKLÖV

This ski jumper found a new way to fly

Gymnastics isn't the only Olympic sport in which athletes fly through the air with the greatest of ease. Nor was Olga Korbut the only Olympian who created a better way to fly! Sometimes, athletes find better ways by accident. Thats what happened to Swedish ski jumper Jan Boklöv *[Yan BUKE-luv]*.

Ever since ski jumping first became a sport in the mid-1800s, most jumpers tried their best to keep their skis straight as they flew through the air. They figured that their oversized skis cut through the wind more smoothly that way. They believed less wind resistance meant more distance.

But during one of Jan's practice jumps, in 1985, a stiff breeze pushed the tips of Jan's skis apart. He was flying through the air with his skis forming the shape of the letter V. Jan was surprised to discover that he seemed steadier in the air while his skis were in that position. He also flew about 15 feet farther than he normally did.

Jan turned the accident into action. He continued to use the V-style in practice and in competition. In 1989, using his new V-style, Jan won the ski-jumping World Cup. Seeing Jan's success, other jumpers began trying the V-style . . . and sticking with it! Today, almost all jumpers use the V-style technique. Because of Jan, the jumpers realized that V is the best route to Victory!

BOBBY ORR

He turned the NHL upside down by changing the way defensemen play their position

Imagine an athlete so talented that an NHL team takes an interest in him at age 14! (The team had to wait until the athlete turned 18 to sign him to a pro contract.) Consider a hockey player so revolutionary that a sportswriter once claimed he changed the very nature of the game.

That athlete was Bobby Orr.

What made Bobby so revolutionary? He was a defenseman who scored goals . . . lots of them! Until he arrived, a defenseman rarely tried to score. A defenseman's job was to protect his team's goal by blocking shots, checking opponents, and clearing the puck. Bobby did all that. But he also used his speed, his puck-handling skill, and his booming slapshot to set up, and score, goals. Before Bobby, no defenseman had ever led the NHL in assists. Bobby led the league in assists five times!

Bobby was known for gathering the puck near center ice, then speeding toward his opponent's goal. Once there, he would either shoot or flick a sharp pass to a teammate. Either way, he struck fear into goalies' hearts and thrilled crowds at the Boston Garden arena.

Bobby played most of his career with the Boston Bruins, and the Bruins recognized his talents early on. He had been playing midget hockey in Parry Sound, Ontario, Canada. He was playing in the Parry Sound Bantam All-Star game. Five NHL scouts were at the game scouting other players, but they noticed Bobby. The scout from the Boston Bruins was particularly impressed with Bobby and told the Bruins what he had seen.

The Bruins wanted to sign Bobby to a contract as soon as he was old enough! Just two years later, Bobby was playing junior hockey on a team with kids as much as eight years older than he was. He averaged 33 goals per season over three years as a teenage defenseman. Those are great numbers for a forward or a center!

A teen sensation

By age 16, Bobby was on the cover of a major Canadian sports magazine. And by 18, he was wearing a Bruin uniform and playing in the NHL.

Bobby made an instant splash his first NHL season (1966-67), scoring 13 goals and winning Rookie of the Year honors. But it was the 1969-70 season that made him a hockey legend. He turned 22 that year, and he turned the NHL on its head. No defenseman had ever led the league in scoring! Bobby did, with 33 goals and 87 assists. He also was the league MVP.

That year, Bobby led Boston to its first Stanley Cup in

29 years, and was named playoff MVP. At the end of the year, *Sports Illustrated* magazine made Bobby the first hockey player ever to be named Sportsman of the Year, and called him the greatest player ever to wear skates.

Bobby played hard, and he collected two main things in his hockey career: records and injuries. He won the Norris Trophy as the NHL's best defenseman a record eight straight times (1968 to 1975) and was the first player to win the NHL MVP award three times in a row (1970 to 1972). In 1971, he set a league record with 102 assists. His best season came in 1974-75, when he scored 46 goals and had 89 assists.

But Bobby paid a price for playing so hard. He broke his shoulder once, busted his nose six times, and, most serious of all, required six operations on his left knee. Sadly, it was the weakness and ongoing pain in his knee that forced Bobby to retire in 1979, at age 30.

The model for all to follow

By the time Bobby was elected to the Hockey Hall of Fame, in 1979, other defensemen were copying his style. Bobby paved the way for other scoring defensemen, like Paul Coffey, Raymond Bourque, and Brian Leetch.

Bobby's NHL records for career scoring by a defenseman (270 goals, 645 assists) stood until the mid-1980's, when New York Islander Denis Potvin broke them. Like every offensive defenseman who came after Bobby, Denis knew what Bobby Orr had meant to hockey. Said Denis: "Bobby was the best. He was the one who came in and changed the game."

STAN MIKITA

He changed the shape of hockey . . . by accident

When Bobby Orr played his final NHL season with the Chicago Blackhawks, in 1979, one of his teammates was another high-scoring superstar: center Stan Mikita. While Bobby had changed the role of the defenseman, Stan had changed the shape of the hockey stick.

And he did it by accident!

In 1968, stick blades were straight, not curved as they are today. Stan had been playing in the league for 10 years, with a straight stick, of course. One day, he had become angry during a practice. To vent his anger, he tried to break his wood stick by jamming it into a crack in the boards. The stick didn't break, but it did bend. Stan kept the bent stick and started shooting pucks with it. He realized the bent stick made the puck easier to maneuver.

Soon, Stan began using the curved stick during games. When he began scoring goals by the bushel, other players bent their sticks, too.

The following season, in 1969-70, the NHL made a rule limiting how much a stick could be curved.

Stan had a long, successful NHL career of 21 years. He led the league in scoring four times and recorded 541 goals and 926 assists. Those are pretty impressive stats. Yet Stan's biggest impact on hockey remains – you guessed it –introducing the curved stick!

DICK FOSBURY

This high jumper discovered that he could be a big success by being a flop!

Dick Fosbury was the greatest flop in Olympic history. And the sport of high jumping hasn't been the same since.

Until Dick arrived on the scene, most high jumpers used the straddle method to clear the bar. The straddle method was also known as the Western roll because the jumper would kick one foot up and then roll over the bar facedown.

When Dick was a sophomore at Medford High School, in Oregon, this was the method he learned, but he wasn't good at it. Dick preferred to use a scissors method of jumping, in which he kicked one foot and then the other over the bar. He did better with that. But he did even better when he developed his own method.

He did that one day in 1963, during a high school meet. Dick had cleared his first jump at 5' 4". He decided that since his hips were usually what knocked the bar off, he would lift his hips more on his next jump. He cleared 5' 6". Then he lifted his hips even more. This made his shoulders go back further, giving him a rather strange look, but it worked. He refined his technique yet again. He would run toward the bar, then turn his back so that he flipped his head and hips over the bar with his back toward the bar. Dick cleared 5' 8". Then he cleared 5' 10". Clearly, he was on to something.

Strange but successful

By the time Dick was a senior in high school, he had developed a whole new style of high jumping. After taking off with his left foot, he flung his body over the bar backward. First, his arched back cleared the bar, then his legs. It was an odd-looking style, but it worked. Dick was 6' 4" tall but he jumped 6' 7" to win the national high school championship.

Dick attended college at Oregon State University. Despite his high school success, Dick's coach kept trying to teach him the straddle style. But after Dick used his flop method to break the Oregon State record with a jump of 6' 10" at a meet in California, his coach said, "That's it. I give up." From then on, they worked to improve Dick's strange but successful style.

The style attracted international attention at the 1968 Summer Olympic Games, in Mexico City, Mexico. Dick set an Olympic and a U.S. record by clearing 7' 4". He won the gold medal, and his jumping style was given a name: the Fosbury Flop.

Dick failed to make the 1972 Olympic team and retired

from track and field. He became a successful civil engineer in Idaho. But his influence on the high-jump event was enormous. Kids around the world began using the Fosbury Flop method that they saw on television.

"I won the gold medal using it," said Dick, and they said, "That looks fun. I want to do that."

Everybody's doing the flop

Soon, those kids were old enough to be Olympic athletes. In 1976, all three medalists used the Fosbury Flop. By 1980, 13 of the 16 high-jump finalists were floppers. Today, thanks to the flop, the world high-jump record is over eight feet.

For taking the high jump to new heights, Dick was inducted into the National Track Hall of Fame and the U.S. Olympic Hall of Fame. "I'm very happy to have given something to the sport," he said.

Even if it was a flop.

TRACK-AND-FIELD CHANGES
New techniques changed shot put and hurdles, too

Dick Fosbury wasn't the first track-and-field athlete who changed his event by inventing his style. In the 1950's, two U.S. athletes won gold medals by combining talent with new techniques.

Before Charles Moore came along, most participants in the 400-meter hurdles took 15 strides between hurdles. But to Charles, 13 strides between leaps seemed smoother and more powerful, and he used that number to dominate the sport.

Other hurdlers did not pick up on the number of steps used by Charles right away. It is easier to change your method of jumping the way Dick Fosbury did than it is to change the way you run an entire 400-meter race. Record books show that hurdlers in 1960 were still using 15 strides.

From 1949 to 1952, Charles was undefeated as a 400-meter hurdler, winning four national intermediate hurdle titles in a row. He won a gold medal in the individual race and a silver medal in the 4 x 400-meter relay at the 1952 Summer Olympics.

At those same Olympic Games, Parry O'Brien won a gold medal in the shot put. Athletes had always relied on strength more than style while throwing the 16-pound iron put (ball). Their technique consisted of hopping sideways, then heaving the shot.

Parry tried a new style, in which he whirled around and threw the shot put, all in one motion. He got the momentum and power of his entire body into the act. And what an act! From 1952 to 1956, Parry won 116 consecutive shot-put competitions, including the one at the 1956 Summer Olympics. By 1959, he held the world record of 63' 4".

The techniques Charles and Parry created were once the exception. Now, they are the rule.

HANK LUISETTI

This ball-handling wizard brought real style and eye-popping moves to basketball

asketball used to be boring. It was a slow game, and there weren't many exciting moves. In fact, there were only two basic shots, the layup and the two-handed set shot. But then, Angelo Hank Luisetti burst onto the scene, and basketball hasn't been the same since.

Hank grew up in San Francisco, California, in the 1920's. As a child, he had to wear painful, awkward leg braces to straighten his legs, but he still loved to play basketball. He was shorter than most of the people he played against, and it was difficult for him to shoot the ball over his taller opponents. So Hank tried something different. He used one hand to loft the ball and the other to guide it. "When I shot with two hands, I couldn't score as well," said Hank. "So I just went to the one hand."

By the time Hank went to college at Stanford University, he had grown to 6' 3". He had become an outstanding basketball player. But it was a famous game on December 30, 1936, that turned Hank Luisetti into a true national star and basketball pioneer.

On that day, the Stanford basketball team took on Long

Island University (LIU) at Madison Square Garden, in New York City. LIU owned a 43-game winning streak until Hank put on a one-man show and led Stanford to a 45–31 victory!

Hank scored 15 of Stanford's 45 points. That was impressive enough. What really stunned the crowd of 17,000 people, though, was Hank's style of play. He made one-handed, leaping, acrobatic shots the likes of which the New York crowd had never seen. He dribbled behind his back. He played every position on the court. He was amazing! When it was over, the crowd gave Hank a standing ovation.

Stanford won the national title the following spring. During Hank's three seasons on the team, Stanford won 68 games and lost only 12. Hank was a three-time All-America and a two-time College Player of the Year. When he graduated, in 1938, he held college basketball records for career points (1,596) and points in a game (50).

Anything is possible

Those records have since been broken, but Hank's effect on hoops continues to grow. Players watched his moves and realized that basketball could be a game of instinct and invention. Coaches decided it was okay to let players show a little style on the court. Basketball players have become more and more creative. The days of the (yawn!) set shot and the (ho-hum!) layup are long gone.

So the next time you see the NBA's Vince Carter slam home a jaw-dropping slam dunk or watch Allen Iverson pull off a crossover dribble, think of Hank Luisetti. He showed the world that anything was possible with a basketball.

KENNY SAILORS
He invented the jumper

When Kenny Sailors grew up in the 1930's, he used a set shot, just like every other player. With his feet on the court, he held the ball chest-high and pushed it toward the basket with both hands. There was only one problem: Kenny's big brother, Bud, always blocked his shot.

Kenny came up with a solution to the problem. He held the ball high over his head with one hand and jumped while shooting the ball. That's right: He used a jump shot, leaping off both feet at the same time, squaring his shoulders to the basket, and letting fly from over his head.

Though historians debate who used the first jumper, many believe that Kenny was the first.

Kenny showed fans his new shot in a big game, just as Hank Luisetti had displayed his revolutionary style in 1936. It was the finals of the 1943 NCAA men's basketball tournament, played at Madison Square Garden in New York City. Kenny scored 16 points and led the University of Wyoming to the championship. He was named MVP of the tournament.

A few years later, NBA stars like Jumpin' Joe Fulks and Paul Arizin perfected the shot even more. Joe averaged 26 points per game in his best season, 1948-49. Paul averaged 22.8 points per game in his 10-year career. They jump-started the jump shot that Kenny had introduced!

GUS DORAIS

The little guy who had a huge impact on football by mastering a new play . . . the forward pass

The University of Notre Dame has produced some of the greatest quarterbacks in football history. Johnny Lujack won two national championships and the 1947 Heisman Trophy. Joe Theismann threw for 528 yards in a college game, and later led the Washington Redskins to a Super Bowl win. Joe Montana led the San Francisco 49ers to four Super Bowl titles. Joe may have been the best of the best.

But the athlete who paved the way for these amazing quarterbacks was another Notre Dame signal-caller. He was Notre Dame's first great quarterback, and his name was Charles "Gus" Dorais [Door-ray].

Gus wasn't big. He stood only 5' 7" and weighed 145 pounds. But he was a four-year starter at quarterback for Notre Dame, from 1910 to 1913. And in his last three seasons, the Fighting Irish didn't lose a single game!

One of those victories turned out to be an unforgettable game in football history. It was November 1, 1913, the day Notre Dame took on the U.S. Military Academy (Army). That day, Notre Dame introduced a weapon that would change the game forever — the forward pass.

In the early days of football, players weren't allowed to pass the ball. It was a game of running with the ball, big pileups . . . and lots of injuries. In fact, football was so brutal that President Teddy Roosevelt threatened to ban the game from college entirely. In response, colleges decided to open up the game to make it less dangerous. In 1906, they legalized the forward pass.

That year, St. Louis University became the first team to use the new play regularly. The team finished the season 11–0 and outscored opponents 407–11! But most coaches at other schools thought the pass was too complicated to be useful. This was especially true of the coaches in the East, where the nation's best college teams were located.

A daring game plan

Notre Dame, which is located in the Midwestern state of Indiana, went undefeated in 1911 and 1912. But it still hadn't faced those top teams in the country. Gus planned to spend the summer of 1913 at a resort in Cedar Point, Ohio. He would be working with his teammate, end Knute Rockne. (Knute, pronounced *Newt*, would later coach Notre Dame to four national championships and become one of the most famous sports figures in the country.) Together, Gus and Knute came up with a game plan.

They brought some footballs along and spent most of their summer practicing and perfecting the forward pass. Footballs were difficult to throw in those days, because the ball was bigger, but Gus learned how to throw a spiral. He practiced moves like rolling out and fading back. He also practiced throwing short, medium, and long passes. In those days, nobody thought of catching the ball on the run. Knute learned to catch it in full stride.

Everyone takes to the air

When the 1913 season began, Notre Dame won its first three games easily, seldom using the pass. But when Notre Dame's Fighting Irish traveled to New York to take on the tough Army squad, it was time for the surprise. It was the first time the Fighting Irish would face one of the powerhouse schools in the East. They were ready.

Gus completed 14 of 17 passes, most of them to Knute. He passed for 243 yards and three touchdowns, as Notre Dame stunned Army, 35–13. The next day, *The New York Times* newspaper ran a huge headline: NOTRE DAME OPEN PLAY AMAZES ARMY. The reporter wrote that the Fighting Irish "flashed the most sensational football ever seen in the East."

That game was the only loss of the season for Army and its coach, Charley Daly. Coach Daly would soon design a passing game of his own. Before long, nearly every team in the country was taking to the air.

Gus became the first Notre Dame player selected to the All-America team. By displaying the power of the forward pass in the East, he assured that it was here to stay.

JACQUES PLANTE

By becoming the first masked man in the NHL, he saved face – his own and those of future goalies

Goaltender Jacques Plante changed the face of hockey. He did it by protecting the faces of goalies!

When Jacques arrived in the National Hockey League, in 1952, goalies didn't wear masks. Many believed a mask would prevent goalies from seeing the ice and the puck clearly. Besides, a mask was considered a sign of weakness.

Jacques played in the NHL for 19 years, 11 of those years for the Montreal Canadiens. In one of his first appearances, he defended the Montreal goal against the Chicago Blackhawks in a semi-final game of the Stanley Cup playoffs. Talk about pressure! It was Game 6 of the semi's and Chicago was leading the series, 3–2. With Jacques in goal, Montreal beat the Blackhawks, 3–0. Montreal won the next game behind Jacques' sparkling goaltending. Over the next several years, Jacques would become one of the best goalies in hockey.

Jacques had thought about wearing a mask during games. He had even experimented with one in practice, but he hadn't dared use one in a game. Hockey players were tough. Who needed face protection — not manly goalies, right?

Then, on November 1, 1959, Jacques dared. During a Canadiens' game against the New York Rangers, a shot hit Jacques just below his left eye. Andy Bathgate, who was a hard shooter, had fired the puck that hit Jacques. Jacques needed seven stitches to close the cut. He was tough and proud, but he wasn't crazy. He told his coach he wouldn't play the rest of the game unless he could wear his mask. When he returned for the next period of play, he had covered his face with a cream-colored mask made of plastic. Coincidentally, a plastics manufacturer had begun making masks for goalies before the start of the season. Jacques had gotten the mask from him.

As the season continued, Jacques kept wearing the mask. He was just as successful with the mask as he had been without it. Other goalies began to realize that wearing a mask actually made it easier to protect the goal. A goalie could keep his eye on the puck for longer periods of time. That was very important in a game in which split-second timing can make all the difference.

The debut of the roving goalie

The mask wasn't the only change that Jacques brought to the NHL. Before Jacques, goalies were taught to always remain in front of the goal. Coaches feared leaving the goal untended, even for a moment. They thought the opposing team could easily score if the goal were open.

Early in his career, Jacques had played for an amateur team that was short on talent. To make up for it, he became a bit of a wanderer. He was a good skater, so he could quickly scramble back to the net in time when he had to.

"I was constantly having to chase the puck behind the net," Jacques told reporters. "Before long I realized that whether the team is bad or good, the goalie can often help himself."

Jacques continued to roam in the NHL, and he continued to star. He recorded the lowest goals-against average in the league every season from 1955-56 through 1959-60. The Canadiens won the Stanley Cup in each of those five years.

A standout goalie, even at 42

During the 1961-62 season, Jacques allowed the fewest goals per game again, and became one of only five goalies ever to earn the Hart Trophy as the league's Most Valuable Player. In all, he led the NHL in goals-against average nine times, a league record. The last time, he was 42 years old.

By the time Jacques retired, in 1975, he had recorded 82 NHL shutouts and 434 wins. More important, he had created an entire generation of goalies who wore masks and roamed away from the goal to help their team. They were simply doing the very same things that had made Jacques a Hall of Famer. After all, why not imitate the best?

DOUG ALLISON

He was the first baseball player to wear a glove

Long before Jacques Plante wore hockey's first goalie mask, Doug Allison took a similar step in baseball. More than 130 years ago, Doug was a catcher on the first pro baseball team in the country, the Cincinnati Red Stockings. Many historians believe he was the first known player to wear a baseball glove.

In the early days, players fielded without gloves. It wasn't considered "manly" to use one. One day in 1869, Doug bruised his hand. To protect the hand, he decided to wear a plain leather glove with the fingers cut off. It had far less padding than the catcher's mitts used today, but it was more than anyone had ever used before. The first known mention in a newspaper of a baseball glove came one year later when Doug wore one.

Most players still shied away from using gloves. Then, in 1877, Albert Spalding, a first baseman for the Chicago Nationals, wore a black finger-less glove. Within 20 years, every major leaguer was wearing a glove.

JULIUS ERVING

Long before Michael Jordan, basketball boasted the high-flying, gravity-defying Dr. J

He couldn't possibly be called by his real name, could he? Julius Winfield Erving II? That didn't sound right. Here was a basketball player with moves that had to be seen to be believed! Clearly, he needed a nickname.

Growing up in Roosevelt, New York, in the 1950's, Julius's friends called him "Jewel" for the way he "glittered" on the court. They tried "The Claw" for the way his enormous hands grabbed every rebound in sight. Finally, they settled on "the doctor." After all, this 6' 7" forward performed a kind of surgery on opposing defenses! A high school teammate capped off the nickname with an initial: J, for Julius. The nickname "Dr. J" stuck.

Julius Erving could soar above the basket in breathtaking fashion. He wasn't the first basketball star to defy gravity. Hall-of-Famers like Elgin Baylor and Connie Hawkins came before him and brought above-the-rim moves to the game. But Julius brought basketball into the modern age. He showed what could happen when players combined superstar skills with style. Because of him, people realized that the best athletes could be artists on the basketball court. And with his bushy Afro, he had an appearance that made fans take notice.

He was Michael's hero

Who did Michael Jordan look up to when he was a kid? That's right . . . Dr. J!

Julius first gained national attention at the University of Massachusetts. From 1968 to 1971 he averaged more than 26 points and 20 rebounds per game. He left college before graduating to sign a pro contract with the Virginia Squires, who played in the American Basketball Association. The ABA was a new league trying to challenge the NBA.

In five years in the ABA (two with Virginia and three with the New York Nets), Julius led the league in scoring three times, was named league MVP three times, and led the Nets to two championships.

Most of the ABA games weren't on television. In fact, pro basketball wasn't nearly as popular in those days as it is today. When Julius did play for a national television audience, fans began to pay attention when the high-flying forward had the ball.

Fans lucky enough to attend the first-ever slam-dunk contest will never forget what they saw. It took place during halftime of the 1976 ABA All-Star Game, in Denver, Colorado. Julius won the competition on his final attempt, when he took off from just inside the free-throw line. He soared his way to the basket and finished off with a jarring slam. No one had ever seen anything like that before.

One coach summed up Dr. J. this way: "I always had the feeling that he would lift off and rise through the glass, out of the arena, and disappear into space."

The pride of Philadelphia

When the ABA and NBA merged, in 1976, four ABA teams — the Denver Nuggets, San Antonio Spurs, New York Nets, and Indiana Pacers — joined the NBA. Julius's contract was sold to the Philadelphia 76ers. He helped the team make it to the NBA Finals in 1977, 1980, 1982, and 1983. In 1983, the 76ers were unstoppable, sweeping every round on the way to winning the NBA title. Julius averaged more than 18 points and seven rebounds during those playoffs. It was Julius's clutch jump shot in Game 4 that clinched the title.

Julius retired in 1987. He had averaged 24.2 points, 8.5 rebounds, 4.2 assists, 1.9 steals, and 1.7 blocked shots per game during his pro career.

By the time Julius retired from pro basketball, his colorful style of play had paved the way for future superstars such as Magic Johnson, Larry Bird, and Michael Jordan. The Doctor had helped make the NBA one of the most popular sports leagues in the world.

SONJA HENIE

This future movie star added grace, ballet and acrobatics to skating – not to mention mini-skirts

Figure skating is one of the most popular sports in the world. Fans love to watch skaters perform their graceful moves and acrobatic jumps to music. The skater who first dazzled the world in this sport was Sonja Henie.

Sonja put the dance and the daring into figure skating. Before her, figure skating routines were mostly just a series of precise, technical moves. She was the first to mix ballet movements, music, and skating. She was a fan of the famous Russian ballerina Anna Pavlova and copied many of the ballerina's moves. (One day, Sonja herself would come to be known as "Pavlova of the Ice.")

Besides adding grace to the sport, Sonja also injected a new level of skill. At 110 pounds, she didn't appear strong, but she was able to perform jumps and spins that were more difficult than any tried before.

As if grace and skill weren't enough to change the sport, Sonja added style! At the time, women skaters wore ankle-length skirts, usually black or another dark color. Not Sonja! She wore a white mini-skirt with fur trim! Fans, and even officials, were completely taken with Sonja.

Sonja was born in Oslo, Norway, on April 8, 1912. She may have inherited her athleticism from her dad, who had been a two-time world amateur bicycling champ in the 1890's. A reporter from *The New York Times* once wrote that Sonja was probably "born with skates on her feet."

Sonja actually received her first set of skates when she was 5 years old. She soon began taking skating lessons. By the time she was 8, she was already the girls' figure-skating champion of Oslo. Within two more years, Sonja was Norway's national skating champ.

An Olympic debut at age 11

In 1924, when she was only 11, Sonja thought she was ready to take on the world! Her coaches must have thought so, too. She participated in the first-ever Winter Olympics, at the time called "International Sports Week," in Chamonix, France. Out of eight skaters, Sonja finished dead last. But the world hadn't seen the last of Sonja!

Sonja returned to Oslo and practiced harder than ever. Her determination paid off. Three years later, in 1927, she won the first of her 10 straight world championships.

The next year, she traveled to St. Moritz, Switzerland, and won her first Olympic gold medal.

In the next two Winter Olympic Games, in 1932 and 1936, Sonja won her second and third gold medals. Only one other woman skater, Katarina Witt of Germany, has even won two gold medals in a row. Sonja had become one of the most famous athletes in the world.

People called Sonja the "Norwegian Doll," but soon they called her something else: a movie star. After retiring from competition at age 24, in 1936, she moved to Hollywood and began making movies.

Her first film, *One in a Million*, was about — what else? — an Olympic skating champion. It was a huge success. Sonja went on to make 10 more movies. Long before Michael Jordan made *Space Jam*, Sonja became one of the first athletes to switch to the silver screen!

When Sonja wasn't making movies, she was starring in her own ice shows. As many as 15 million people watched her perform between 1937 and 1947. Through her skill and style as a skater, her fame as a movie star, and her exciting shows, Sonja inspired thousands of young women to take up figure skating.

She was a different kind of skater, and since Sonja Henie, the sport hasn't been the same.

PETE GOGOLAK

He started a revolution in the NFL when he introduced soccer-style kicking

In 1963, NFL kickers made fewer than half of their field-goal attempts. By 1973, most NFL kickers were making nearly two out of every three field-goal attempts! What had happened? Almost all kickers had started using the kicking style Pete Gogolak introduced. Football was never the same after Pete!

When Pete tried out for his high school football team, as a sophomore in 1957, he wasn't sure what he was getting himself into. He had recently arrived from Hungary, his native land in Europe, and he didn't know a thing about football.

"I didn't even know that football involved any kicking," said Pete. "To me, it was a bunch of guys who huddled together, whispered things in each other's ears, lined up, and then hit each other. "

Pete had been a star soccer player in Budapest, Hungary. But when Russian tanks invaded the country to suppress the 1956 Hungarian Revolution, the Gogolaks decided they had to leave Hungary. So Pete, his parents, and his younger brother, Charlie, walked

15 miles under cover of darkness to escape into Austria. Soon, the Gogolak family made its way to the United States, settling in Ogdensburg, New York. Pete was heartbroken — not because he was thousands of miles from home, but because his high school had no soccer team. Pete decided to join the football team, instead.

On the day before the team's first game, the coach began a search for a placekicker. One by one, Pete's teammates tried to kick field goals. For their approach to the ball, they all lined up several yards straight behind the holder. That's the way kickers had been lining up for years. Then Pete volunteered to try — only he lined up at an angle, to the side of the ball. "I'll never forget the frightened expression on my holder's face," Pete recalled.

Booting the ball and becoming a starter

Instead of kicking the ball with his toes, Pete swung his right instep into it, soccer-style. The ball traveled 40 yards but under the crossbar. Pete wasn't discouraged, though.

He practiced constantly and, eventually, became his team's starting kicker. He tried three field goals in his high school career and made two of them.

Once he got to college, though, Pete showed that he — and his soccer-style kicking — were something special. In his first game, for Cornell University, Pete booted three field goals, including a 48-yarder! During his senior season, he kicked a 50-yard field goal, the longest in the nation. From 1961 to 1963, Pete also connected on 54 of 55 extra-point attempts, including a record 44 in a row.

After college, Pete was drafted by the Buffalo Bills of the old American Football League. He collected 217 points and two league championships in his first two seasons. Despite his success, many teammates remained uncomfortable with his kicking style. In fact, Buffalo's usual holder, quarterback Jack Kemp, refused to hold the ball for Pete. He let the backup quarterback do it.

It would take awhile, but eventually, Pete's kicking style had to be accepted by everyone because it was working so well. Pete signed a contract with the NFL's New York Giants before his third season. In eight of his nine years with the Giants, he led the team in scoring. In 1965, his 28 field goals led the league. Pete retired as the Giant's all-time leading scorer.

By then, there were several soccer-style kickers in the league, including Pete's brother, Charlie, who attended Princeton University. The Washington Redskins drafted Charlie in the first round, which was unheard of for a kicker. Charlie was a fine kicker as well. He played in the NFL for six seasons and scored 270 points in his 55-game career.

Today, every placekicker in the NFL boots soccer-style. After fleeing the Hungarian Revolution, Pete had started a revolution of his own!

TRENDSETTERS

Numbered uniforms, white shoes, long nails, and knickers all were fashion statements

Sometimes it's not athletes' actions alone that make them stand out. Sometimes, their style of dress is as unique as — or *more* unique than — their style of play. The following people were fashion pioneers. Just by walking onto the playing field, they dared to be different.

THE YANKS' BACKS

In 1929, the New York Yankees became the first major league team to wear numbers on the backs of their uniform jerseys. They did it so that each player could be easily identified. Thirteen years earlier, the Cleveland Indians had begun wearing numbers — on their sleeves.

The Yankee players were numbered according to their spot in the batting order. That's why Babe Ruth became famous as number 3 and Lou Gehrig became famous as number 4.

BIG KLU'S UNIFORM

Cincinnati Red first baseman Ted Kluszewski was a big guy. He was 6' 2", weighed 225 pounds, and swung a heavy 38-ounce bat during his 15 years as a major league first baseman. In 1954, his best season, "Big Klu" led the National League with 49 homers and 141 runs batted in.

But Ted's bulging biceps made it uncomfortable to wear his team jersey. "We had those flannel uniforms, and every time I'd swing the bat, my arms would get hung up on the sleeves," Ted told the *Cincinnati Enquirer* newspaper.

Ted complained to the Reds' bosses about the tight sleeves, but they offered no solution. So one day, he simply took a pair of scissors and cut off the sleeves! "They got pretty upset," Ted remembered, "but it was either that or change my swing. And I wasn't going to change my swing."

Ted became famous for his sleeveless look. When the Reds retired his number, in 1998, they displayed a nine-foot jersey behind the leftfield wall. There was Big Klu's familiar number 18 . . . with no sleeves!

JOE WILLIE'S WHITE SHOES

Joseph William Namath, the great New York Jet quarterback of the 1960's, was famous for doing his own thing. Joe Willie, as he was sometimes called, grew a Fu Manchu mustache (the ends of the 'stache drooped down). He starred in a television commercial for panty hose. He wrote a book about himself that was called *I Can't Wait Until Tomorrow 'Cause I Get Better Looking Every Day!* And he wore white football cleats when everyone else was wearing black ones.

Joe was the most famous athlete in New York, and he earned the nickname "Broadway Joe." He was certainly different — and courageous, too. When the Jets were 19-point underdogs against the Baltimore Colts in the 1969 Super Bowl, Joe guaranteed to reporters that his team would win. And it did, 16–7!

PISTOL PETE'S SOCKS

"Pistol Pete" Maravich was the greatest scorer in college basketball history. He led the nation in scoring in each of his three varsity seasons (1968 to 1970) at Louisiana State University, and averaged more than 44 points per game. No college player has ever scored more points, not even stars who played *four* varsity seasons. Pete also spent 10 years in the NBA, making four All-Star teams.

Pete was known for fancy passes, frequent shots, and floppy socks. While most of his fellow players wore tight white socks, Pete wore loose gray ones. He looked as if he were wearing scarves around his ankles! Pete's socks were important to him. He would wash and dry them in his dormitory after each time he wore them. Nobody dared to copy Pete's style, on his ankles or on the court!

FLOJO'S FASHIONS

Florence Griffith Joyner, known to her fans as "FloJo," was the fastest woman on the planet in 1988. That year, she shattered the world record by running 100 meters in 10.49 seconds at the U.S. Olympic Trials. At the Olympics, she won three gold medals and set a record in the 200-meter dash.

Besides being known for her speed, FloJo was famous for her clothing style. She designed her own running clothes, including bodysuits, which no one had seen on a runner before. At the Olympic trials, she wore unitards in bright colors that had one leg covered and one leg bare! She also wore leggings with lace insets along the outside of the leg. FloJo grew her fingernails four inches long and decorated them to go with the bright colors of her racing outfits.

PAYNE'S PLUS-FOURS

Until Tiger Woods became world famous, Payne Stewart was probably the most recognizable person on the golf course. It wasn't because he won three major titles, two U.S. Opens, and one PGA championship.

It was because of the way he *dressed*.

Payne dressed like a classy old-time golfer. He wore knickers, which are pants that end just below the knee. The kind he wore are called plus-fours because they are four inches longer than regular knickers. He wore hats called tam-o'-shanters, small, round caps with a pompon in the center. He also wore fancy golf shoes. One pair was lavender snakeskin with brass toes and heel plates.

In 1982, after noticing that he was dressed just like every other golfer on the course, he made a decision.

"I vowed right then I was not going to be another look-alike," Payne told *Sports Illustrated*.

WANT TO HAVE MORE FUN

WITH SPORTS ILLUSTRATED FOR KIDS?

GET A FREE TRIAL ISSUE of SPORTS ILLUSTRATED FOR KIDS **magazine.** Each monthly issue is jam-packed with awesome athletes, super-sized photos, cool sports facts, comics, games, and jokes!

Ask your mom or dad to call and order your free trial issue today! The phone number is 1-800-732-5080.

PLUG IN TO www.sikids.com. That's the S.I. FOR KIDS website on the Internet. You'll find great games, free fantasy leagues, sports news, trivia quizzes, and more.

CHECK OUT S.I. FOR KIDS **Weekly** in the comic section of many newspapers. It has lots of cool photos, stories, and puzzles from the Number 1 sports magazine for kids!

LOOK FOR more S.I. FOR KIDS **books.** They make reading **fun!**